THE SUNKEN GARDEN
AND OTHER POEMS

THE SUNKEN GARDEN
AND OTHER POEMS

WALTER DE LA MARE

wildsidepress.com

WILDSIDE PRESS

Originally published in 1902.
Published by Wildside Press LLC.
wildsidepress.com

CONTENTS

THE LITTLE SALAMANDER

TO MARGOT

WHEN I GO FREE,
I think 'twill be
A night of stars and snow,
And the wild fires of frost shall light
My footsteps as I go;
Nobody—nobody will be there
With groping touch, or sight,
To see me in my bush of hair
Dance burning through the night.

THE SUNKEN GARDEN

SPEAK NOT—WHISPER NOT;
Here bloweth thyme and bergamot;
Softly on the evening hour,
Secret herbs their spices shower,
Dark-spiked rosemary and myrrh,
Lean-stalked, purple lavender;
Hides within her bosom, too,
All her sorrows, bitter rue.
Breathe not—trespass not;
Of this green and darkling spot,
Latticed from the moon's beams,
Perchance a distant dreamer dreams;
Perchance upon its darkening air,
The unseen ghosts of children fare,
Faintly swinging, sway and sweep,
Like lovely sea-flowers in its deep;
While, unmoved, to watch and ward,
'Mid its gloom'd and daisied sward,
Stands with bowed and dewy head
That one little leaden Lad.

THE RIDDLERS

'THOU SOLITARY!' the Blackbird cried,
'I, from the happy Wren,
Linnet and Blackcap, Woodlark, Thrush,
Perched all upon a sweetbrier bush,
Have come at cold of midnight-tide
To ask thee, Why and when
Grief smote thy heart so thou dost sing
In solemn hush of evening,
So sorrowfully, lovelorn Thing—
Nay, nay, not sing, but rave, but wail,
Most melancholic Nightingale?
Do not the dews of darkness steep
All pinings of the day in sleep?
Why, then, when rocked in starry nest
We mutely couch, secure, at rest,
Doth thy lone heart delight to make
Music for sorrow's sake?'
A Moon was there. So still her beam,
It seemed the whole world lay a-dream,
Lulled by the watery sea.
And from her leafy night-hung nook
Upon this stranger soft did look
The Nightingale: sighed he:—
''Tis strange, my friend; the Kingfisher
But yestermorn conjured me here
Out of his green and gold to say
Why thou, in splendour of the noon
Wearest of colour but golden shoon.
And else dost thee array
In a most sombre suit of black?
"Surely," he sighed, "some load of grief,

Past all our thinking—and belief—
Must weigh upon his back!"
Do, then, in turn, tell me,—If joy
Thy heart as well as voice employ,
Why dost thou now, most Sable, shine
In plumage woefuller far than mine?
Thy silence is a sadder thing
Than any dirge I sing!'
Thus then these two small birds, perched there,
Breathed a strange riddle both did share
Yet neither could expound.
And we—who sing but as we can,
In the small knowledge of a man—
Have we an answer found?
Nay, some are happy whose delight
Is hid even from themselves from sight;
And some win peace who spend
The skill of words to sweeten despair
Of finding consolation where
Life has but one dark end;
Who, in rapt solitude, tell o'er
A tale as lovely as forlore
Into the midnight air.

MRS. GRUNDY

'STEP VERY SOFTLY, sweet Quiet-foot,
Stumble not, whisper not, smile not:
By this dark ivy stoop cheek and brow.
Still even thy heart! What seest thou?'
'High coifed, broad-browed, aged, suave yet grim,
A large flat face, eyes keenly dim,
Staring at nothing—that's me!—and yet,
With a hate one could never, no, never forget....'
'This is my world, my garden, my home,
Hither my father bade mother to come
And bear me out of the dark into light,
And happy I was in her tender sight.
'And then, thou frail flower, she died and went,
Forgetting my pitiless banishment,
And that Old Woman—an Aunt—she said,
Came hither, lodged, fattened, and made her bed.
'Oh yes, thou most blessed, from Monday to Sunday
Has lived on me, preyed on me, Mrs. Grundy:
Called me, "dear Nephew"; on each of those chairs
Has gloated in righteousness, heard my prayers.
'Why didst thou dare the thorns of the grove,
Timidest trespasser, huntress of love?
Now thou has peeped, and now dost know
What kind of creature is thine for foe.
'Not that she'll tear out thy innocent eyes,
Poison thy mouth with deviltries.
Watch thou, wait thou: soon will begin
The guile of a voice: hark!... "Come in, Come in!"'

THE DARK HOUSE

SEE THIS HOUSE, how dark it is
Beneath its vast-boughed trees!
Not one trembling leaflet cries
To that Watcher in the skies—
'Remove, remove thy searching gaze,
Innocent, of Heaven's ways,
Brood not, Moon, so wildly bright,
On secrets hidden from sight.'
'Secrets,' sighs the night-wind,
'Vacancy is all I find;
Every keyhole I have made
Wail a summons, faint and sad,
No voice ever answers me,
Only vacancy.'
'Once, once ...' the cricket shrills,
And far and near the quiet fills
With its tiny voice, and then
Hush falls again.
Mute shadows creeping slow
Mark how the hours go,
Every stone is mouldering slow,
And the least winds that blow
Some minutest atom shake,
Some fretting ruin make
In roof and walls. How black it is
Beneath these thick-boughed trees!

MISTRESS FELL

'WHOM seek you here, sweet Mistress Fell?'
'One who loved me passing well.
Dark his eye, wild his face—
Stranger, if in this lonely place
Bide such an one, then, prythee, say
I am come here to-day.'
'Many his like, Mistress Fell?'
'I did not look, so cannot tell.
Only this I surely know,
When his voice called me, I must go;
Touched me his fingers, and my heart
Leapt at the sweet pain's smart.'
'Why did he leave you, Mistress Fell?'
'Magic laid its dreary spell.—
Stranger, he was fast asleep;
Into his dream I tried to creep;
Called his name, soft was my cry:
He answered—not one sigh.
'The flower and the thorn are here;
Falleth the night-dew, cold and clear;
Out of her bower the bird replies,
Mocking the dark with ecstasies:
See how the earth's green grass doth grow,
Praising what sleeps below!
'Thus have they told me. And I come,
As flies the wounded wild-bird home.
Not tears I give; but all that he
Clasped in his arms sweet charity;
All that he loved—to him I bring
For a close whispering.'

THE STRANGER

In THE WOODS AS I DID WALK,
Dappled with the moon's beam,
I did with a Stranger talk,
And his name was Dream.
Spurred his heel, dark his cloak,
Shady-wide his bonnet's brim;
His horse beneath a silvery oak
Grazed as I talked with him.
Softly his breast-brooch burned and shone;
Hill and deep were in his eyes;
One of his hands held mine, and one
The fruit that makes men wise.
Wonderly strange was earth to see,
Flowers white as milk did gleam;
Spread to Heaven the Assyrian Tree
Over my head with Dream.
Dews were still betwixt us twain;
Stars a trembling beauty shed;
Yet—not a whisper comes again
Of the words he said.

THE FLIGHT

HOW DO THE DAYS press on, and lay
Their fallen locks at evening down,
Whileas the stars in darkness play
And moonbeams weave a crown—
A crown of flower-like light in heaven,
Where in the hollow arch of space
Morn's mistress dreams, and the Pleiads seven
Stand watch about her place.
Stand watch—O days no number keep
Of hours when this dark clay is blind.
When the world's clocks are dumb in sleep
'Tis then I seek my kind.

THE REMONSTRANCE

I WAS AT PEACE UNTIL YOU CAME
And set a careless mind aflame;
I lived in quiet; cold, content;
All longing in safe banishment,
Until your ghostly lips and eyes
Made wisdom unwise.
Naught was in me to tempt your feet
To seek a lodging. Quite forgot
Lay the sweet solitude we two
In childhood used to wander through;
Time's cold had closed my heart about;
And shut you out.
Well, and what then?... O vision grave,
Take all the little all I have!
Strip me of what in voiceless thought
Life's kept of life, unhoped, unsought!—
Reverie and dream that memory must
Hide deep in dust!
This only I say,—Though cold and bare
The haunted house you have chosen to share,
Still 'neath its walls the moonbeam goes
And trembles on the untended rose;
Still o'er its broken roof-tree rise
The starry arches of the skies;
And 'neath your lightest word shall be
The thunder of an ebbing sea.

THE EXILE

I AM that Adam who, with Snake for guest,
Hid anguished eyes upon Eve's piteous breast.
I am that Adam who, with broken wings,
Fled from the Seraph's brazen trumpetings.
Betrayed and fugitive, I still must roam
A world where sin—and beauty—whisper of home.
Oh, from wide circuit, shall at length I see
Pure daybreak lighten again on Eden's tree?
Loosed from remorse and hope and love's distress,
Enrobe me again in my lost nakedness?
No more with wordless grief a loved one grieve,
But to heaven's nothingness re-welcome Eve?

EYES

O STRANGE DEVICES that alone divide
The seër from the seen—
The very highway of earth's pomp and pride
That lies between
The traveller and the cheating, sweet delight
Of where he longs to be,
But which, bound hand and foot, he, close on night,
Can only see.

THE TRYST

WHY IN MY HEART, O GRIEF,
Dost thou in beauty bide?
Dead is my well-content,
And buried deep my pride.
Cold are their stones, beloved,
To hand and side.
The shadows of even are gone,
Shut are the day's clear flowers,
Now have her birds left mute
Their singing bowers,
Lone shall we be, we twain,
In the night hours.
Thou with thy cheek on mine,
And dark hair loosed, shalt see
Take the far stars for fruit
The cypress tree,
And in the yew's black
Shall the moon be.
We will tell no old tales,
Nor heed if in wandering air
Die a lost song of love
Or the once fair;
Still as well-water be
The thoughts we share!
And, while the ghosts keep
Tryst from chill sepulchres,
Dreamless our gaze shall sleep,
And sealed our ears;
Heart unto heart will speak,
Without tears.
O, thy veiled, lovely face—

Joy's strange disguise—
Shall be the last to fade
From these rapt eyes,
Ere the first dart of daybreak
Pierce the skies.

THE OLD MEN

OLD AND ALONE, SIT WE,
Caged, riddle-rid men;
Lost to earth's 'Listen!' and 'See!'
Thought's 'Wherefore?' and 'When?'
Only far memories stray
Of a past once lovely, but now
Wasted and faded away,
Like green leaves from the bough.
Vast broods the silence of night,
The ruinous moon
Lifts on our faces her light,
Whence all dreaming is gone.
We speak not; trembles each head;
In their sockets our eyes are still;
Desire as cold as the dead;
Without wonder or will.
And One, with a lanthorn, draws near,
At clash with the moon in our eyes:
'Where art thou?' he asks: 'I am here,'
One by one we arise.
And none lifts a hand to withhold
A friend from the touch of that foe:
Heart cries unto heart, 'Thou art old!'
Yet reluctant, we go.

THE FOOL'S SONG

NEVER, NO, NEVER, listen too long,
To the chattering wind in the willows, the night bird's song.
'Tis sad in sooth to lie under the grass,
But none too gladsome to wake and grow cold where life's shadows pass.
Dumb the old Toll-Woman squats,
And, for every green copper battered and worn, doles out Nevers and Nots.
I know a Blind Man, too,
Who with a sharp ear listens and listens the whole world through.
Oh, sit we snug to our feast,
With platter and finger and spoon—and good victuals at least.

THE DREAMER

O THOU who giving helm and sword,
Gav'st, too, the rusting rain,
And starry dark's all tender dews
To blunt and stain:
Out of the battle I am sped,
Unharmed, yet stricken sore;
A living shape 'mid whispering shades
On Lethe's shore.
No trophy in my hands I bring,
To this sad, sighing stream,
The neighings and the trumps and cries
Were but a dream—a dream.
Traitor to life, of life betrayed—
O, of thy mercy deep,
A dream my all, the all I ask
Is sleep.

MOTLEY

COME, Death, I'd have a word with thee;
And thou, poor Innocency;
And Love—a lad with broken wing;
And Pity, too:
The Fool shall sing to you,
As Fools will sing.
Ay, music hath small sense,
And a tune's soon told,
And Earth is old,
And my poor wits are dense;
Yet have I secrets,—dark, my dear,
To breathe you all: Come near.
And lest some hideous listener tells,
I'll ring my bells.
They're all at war!—
Yes, yes, their bodies go
'Neath burning sun and icy star
To chaunted songs of woe,
Dragging cold cannon through a mire
Of rain and blood and spouting fire,
The new moon glinting hard on eyes
Wide with insanities!
Hush!... I use words
I hardly know the meaning of;
And the mute birds
Are glancing at Love
From out their shade of leaf and flower,
Trembling at treacheries
Which even in noonday cower.
Heed, heed not what I said
Of frenzied hosts of men,

More fools than I,
On envy, hatred fed,
Who kill, and die—
Spake I not plainly, then?
Yet Pity whispered, 'Why?'
Thou silly thing, off to thy daisies go.
Mine was not news for child to know,
And Death—no ears hath. He hath supped where creep
Eyeless worms in hush of sleep;
Yet, when he smiles, the hand he draws
Athwart his grinning jaws—
Faintly the thin bones rattle, and—There, there;
Hearken how my bells in the air
Drive away care!...
Nay, but a dream I had
Of a world all mad.
Not simple happy mad like me,
Who am mad like an empty scene
Of water and willow tree,
Where the wind hath been;
But that foul Satan-mad,
Who rots in his own head,
And counts the dead,
Not honest one—and two—
But for the ghosts they were,
Brave, faithful, true,
When head in air,
In Earth's clear green and blue
Heaven they did share
With Beauty who bade them there....
There, now! Death goes—
Mayhap I've wearied him.
Ay, and the light doth dim,
And asleep 's the rose,
And tired Innocence
In dreams is hence....
Come, Love, my lad,
Nodding that drowsy head,
'Tis time thy prayers were said!

TO E.T.: 1917

YOU SLEEP TOO WELL—too far away,
For sorrowing word to soothe or wound;
Your very quiet seems to say
How longed-for a peace you have found.
Else, had not death so lured you on,
You would have grieved—'twixt joy and fear—
To know how my small loving son
Had wept for you, my dear.

ALEXANDER

IT WAS THE GREAT ALEXANDER,
Capped with a golden helm,
Sate in the ages, in his floating ship,
In a dead calm.
Voices of sea-maids singing
Wandered across the deep:
The sailors labouring on their oars
Rowed, as in sleep.
All the high pomp of Asia,
Charmed by that siren lay,
Out of their weary and dreaming minds,
Faded away.
Like a bold boy sate their Captain,
His glamour withered and gone,
In the souls of his brooding mariners,
While the song pined on.
Time like a falling dew,
Life like the scene of a dream
Laid between slumber and slumber,
Only did seem....
O Alexander, then,
In all us mortals too,
Wax thou not bold—too bold
On the wave dark-blue!
Come the calm, infinite night,
Who then will hear
Aught save the singing
Of the sea-maids clear?

FOR ALL THE GRIEF

FOR all the grief I have given with words
May now a few clear flowers blow,
In the dust, and the heat, and the silence of birds,
Where the lonely go.
For the thing unsaid that heart asked of me
Be a dark, cool water calling—calling
To the footsore, benighted, solitary,
When the shadows are falling.
O, be beauty for all my blindness,
A moon in the air where the weary wend,
And dews burdened with loving-kindness
In the dark of the end.

FAREWELL

WHEN I lie where shades of darkness
Shall no more assail mine eyes,
Nor the rain make lamentation
When the wind sighs;
How will fare the world whose wonder
Was the very proof of me?
Memory fades, must the remembered
Perishing be?
Oh, when this my dust surrenders
Hand, foot, lip, to dust again,
May these loved and loving faces
Please other men!
May the rusting harvest hedgerow
Still the Traveller's Joy entwine,
And as happy children gather
Posies once mine.
Look thy last on all things lovely,
Every hour. Let no night
Seal thy sense in deathly slumber
Till to delight
Thou have paid thy utmost blessing;
Since that all things thou wouldst praise
Beauty took from those who loved them
In other days.

CLEAR EYES

CLEAR EYES do dim at last,
And cheeks outlive their rose.
Time, heedless of the past,
No loving-kindness knows;
Chill unto mortal lip
Still Lethe flows.
Griefs, too, but brief while stay,
And sorrow, being o'er,
Its salt tears shed away,
Woundeth the heart no more.
Stealthily lave those waters
That solemn shore.
Ah, then, sweet face burn on,
While yet quick memory lives!
And Sorrow, ere thou art gone,
Know that my heart forgives—
Ere yet, grown cold in peace,
It loves not, nor grieves.

MUSIC

WHEN music sounds, gone is the earth I know,
And all her lovely things even lovelier grow;
Her flowers in vision flame, her forest trees,
Lift burdened branches, stilled with ecstasies.
When music sounds, out of the water rise
Naiads whose beauty dims my waking eyes,
Rapt in strange dream burns each enchanted face,
With solemn echoing stirs their dwelling-place.
When music sounds, all that I was I am
Ere to this haunt of brooding dust I came;
While from Time's woods break into distant song
The swift-winged hours, as I hasten along.

IN A CHURCHYARD

As children bidden to go to bed
Puff out their candle's light,
Since that the natural dark is best
For them to take their flight
Into the realm of sleep: so we
God's bidding did obey;
Not without fear our tired eyes shut,
And wait—and wait—the day.

TWO HOUSES

IN THE STRANGE CITY OF LIFE
Two houses I know well:
One wherein Silence a garden hath,
And one where Dark doth dwell.
Roof unto roof they stand,
Shadowing the dizzied street,
Where Vanity flaunts her gilded booths
In the noontide glare and heat.
Green-graped upon their walls
The ancient, hoary vine
Hath clustered their carven lichenous stones
With tendril serpentine.
And ever and anon,
Dazed in that clamorous throng,
I thirst for the soundless fount that stills
Those orchards mute of song.
Knock, knock! nor knock in vain.
Heart, all thy secrets tell
Where Silence a fast-sealed garden hath
Where Dark doth dwell.

www.ingramcontent.com/pod-product-compliance
Lightning Source LLC
Chambersburg PA
CBHW010039040426
42331CB00037B/3352